BEYOND
OLD AGE

Essays on Living and Dying

ANNEMARIE ROEPER, ED.D.

Azalea Art Press
Berkeley . CA

ISBN: 978-0-9829541-9-5

Front Cover Art:
Franz Marc
Die grossen blauen Pferde
(The Large Blue Horses)
1911 / oil on canvas
Collection Walker Art Center, Minneapolis
Gift of the T. B. Walker Foundation,
Gilbert M. Walker Fund, 1942

Back Cover Photo:
Shoey Sindel

Acknowledgements:

Growing Old Gifted
originally appeared in
The "I" of the Beholder,
by Annemarie Roeper, Ed.D.
with Ann Higgins,
Great Potential Press, 2007.

DEDICATION:

*I dedicate this book to
the children of the world,
whose trust we must
strive to honor.*

CONTENTS

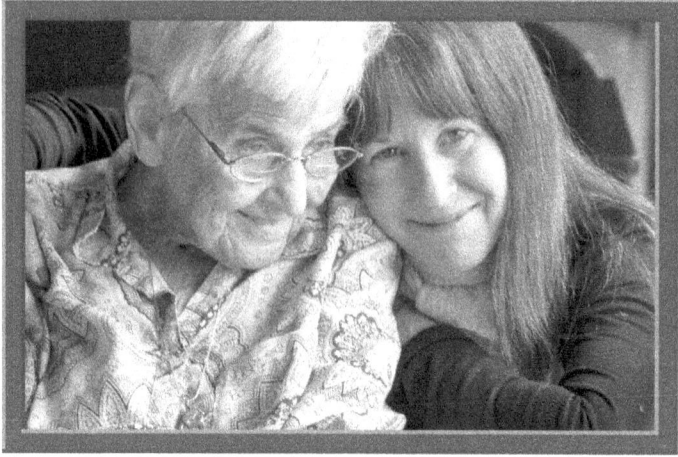

Annemarie
& Karen Mireau

Publisher's Note:

These provocative and insightful essays on the universal challenges of aging were written by Annemarie Roeper from the ages of 87 to 92.

Perceptiveness, originality of thought and the ability to put into crystalline prose the most tender, unspoken chords of our human being have always been the hallmarks of Annemarie's work.

These qualities were amplified to an even higher degree during the writing of these essays, marking a new and invigorating stage in her career as an educator and as a highly creative thinker and writer.

I have immense gratitude for having been allowed to participate in the birthing of this book and it is with immeasurable joy that I now share Annemarie's inspiring words with you.

- Karen Mireau

INTRODUCTION:

On a clear day, from Annemarie's bedroom window there is an impressive view of the Golden Gate Bridge. The view is significant because Annemarie relies on her exterior landscape as an aid in exploring her interior landscape. She has the ability to craft an emotional structure that spans these opposites. Reading the words of Annemarie Roeper is a call to experience this liminal space -- the transitional place where worlds converge -- the bridge between the familiar and unfamiliar.

In this noteworthy collection of essays on aging, Annemarie also moves us to the paradoxical space between affective and cognitive and rouses us to action or reaction. In this way she is able to create a bond that invites us to intimacy. With Annemarie's genuine ability to express her development there is recognition of her vulnerability and openness, which she offers as a gift of friendship. She understands that we, too, will be facing these same concerns and she offers her process as means of self exploration. As she tells her story she demonstrates a willingness to accept the landscape as it is and displays a spirit of adventure in exploring the terrain.

Annemarie is able to share her journey "beyond old age" with deep feelings and honest emotions as well as keen insight and remarkable thoughtfulness. It is her ability to make the connection between thinking and feeling that creates complexity and authenticity. The reader is pulled along with vigorous agreement or disagreement -- at times arguing with her forcefully or moved to tears with shared recognition. Annemarie's words are compelling and require that we both think and feel along with her despite our own personal agenda.

While "embracing the mystery" Annemarie zigzags from dependence to independence, from life to death, from action to reflection, from constancy to change, from imagination to reality and then back again. She provides her unique perspective as her view changes. In revisiting these same themes the layers of meaning surface and new understandings materialize. Concurrently as life events take place there is an unfolding of emotions that continues to transform Annemarie's life and she presents these ideas for further exploration.

The ideas linger and Annemarie encourages us to revisit them along with her. She demonstrates a quiet courage with her investigations and as she steps to the edge she provides room for us alongside her. She does not resist exploring the places that are unpleasant or unexpected and shares her struggles while providing compassion and hope. She creates a lively place that exists where love meets fear and reality meets the unknown. She entices us with her ideas and tempts us to try them on for size. Let her know how they fit.

- MICHELE KANE, ED.D.

ANNEMARIE, AGE 92

PREFACE:

In a long life like mine you begin to think that nothing
new could ever happen again, and yet I know that the
greatest unpredictability is still ahead of me. I am
anticipating with great curiosity and anxiety that which I
can't anticipate. My hope is that these pages might
prepare some future elders for the challenges of the
greatest unknown that is still ahead of them; namely,
death and all that it entails.

I seem to have a need to be totally honest with myself. Is
there a God? Is there a guiding force? In some way, I
believe my life has always been guided and protected, but
what that is I may never know. Much as I have learned
and have almost been forced to find answers, I know I
may not find them. Learning about letting go of control is
the essence of this stage of life.

Writing this book has given me a different perception of
the continuity in my life. It has helped me to put a

framework around the consistency as well as the changes.

It has also opened my eyes to the fact that I have begun a new chapter, one that I might entitle, "The Experience of Never-Agains."

The fact remains that I have to live with the unknown and die with the unknown. Fortunately, love and joy and the warmth of family, friendship and the beauty of nature are also a very substantial part of the mystery of this life. Perhaps I need to end by saying that we need to have faith in that mystery. That alone may be the greatest wisdom the world has to offer us.

ANNEMARIE, AGE 18 MONTHS
WITH HER MOTHER
GERTRUD (WIENER) BONDY

GROWING OLD GIFTED

There are many stories about old people: about their surprising longevity and their ability to continue to participate in social life -- in other words, how they stay young; but not much about how they actually grow old. I don't really know what old age is anymore or when it begins. I've seen many people get old and die. What comes after adulthood? Seniorhood? Isn't that just an older adult? What defines a senior?

What a difference between my grandparents at age 70 and my generation at age 70! When my mother was 70, it was like today's 80. Getting old and dying kept being postponed. I used to think that old age began about age 70. And so it did, but right along with my own aging, people began to stay younger older, or did they get older older? Well, I am too old to figure that out! It was as though the end of the road moved further and further away as I traveled it. Being an "adult" covered an ever-larger span of time. People in their 70s are fully functioning adults, often deeply rooted in the only reality we know.

There is little inclination to ponder life, death, and eternity, with which mankind is eternally concerned. We have a tendency to postpone these thoughts until we are closer to our deathbed, because often, especially in older old age, we need to devote our attention to daily (or immediate) survival. But upon arrival in one's early 80s, the road one has been traveling, which, up until now had been relatively well lit, well described, and well worn, begins to peter out, until one is left standing in a field, no longer sure of the way.

Older old age has not been well described except as a lack of young age. Now that I am 87, I am feeling that I'm kind of on virgin ground, and there is not much that can help me and others cope with these experiences. Most of what I read and observe is based on the idea of staying young as long as we can. While the adolescent is looking forward to being grown up, the old person is trying hard to remain at the stage of the fully capable and participating adult. Much of what I'll call older old age consists of cumulative losses. You may lose your spouse, your friends and relatives (many of whom you've known all your life); many of your capacities diminish, such as your eyesight, your hearing, your sense of smell. At some point you lose your driver's license and you lose at least some of your memory. You also lose status and respect.

Old age is a time of loss; it can't be denied -- it should not be denied. Many try in diverse ways to hold on with all their might to their past status. It is also a time when people begin to get confused. I feel the confusion might be part of the denial, "If I can no longer really understand the loss, it may not hurt so much." I personally want to experience this period with open eyes. In our society you don't really count anymore once you pass into older old age. You feel demoted. This is a huge problem, and typical for our society. The rug seems pulled out from under our feet. I am elaborating on this because I am literally in the middle of this experience.

How do you find yourself in older old age? Rather, how do you find your new position in life? Is it a new period of dependency? Or is it in some way a repetition of childhood, only instead of having a growing body, geared toward attaining independence, you have a disintegrating body, and you don't know how far you are yet going to sink. When you are a child you look forward to building up, to gaining. In older old age, you don't know how far the deterioration is going to go, and if you are gifted you stand by it with open eyes.

When we're younger, we learn to compensate for almost everything in which we may become deficient. We can try to fix what ever may be wrong. We can fix relationships, for instance, by trying harder. We may say, "Well, if I don't get to Timbuktu this year, I can always go later." As we get older, we can't continue to compensate for everything that we might lose. We give up one thing after another, and we have to admit to ourselves that we can't repair it anymore. What we need to do is to find a way of facing the ongoing losses, and learn how to cope with that fact, rather than compensate.

Many people find ways of accepting the losses by putting them into a religious framework ("It's God's will.") One of the ways in which all of us have to cope with life is to look at whatever happens in a most honest way, not necessarily finding ways in which to cover up these losses, or in which to compensate for them. Maybe that's the task of the older old person -- to look at things as they are, without trying to compensate or replace them. I will never be young again. I will never drive a car again. My life on this planet is definitely moving toward its very end. This is probably the last stage of my life. Some of my dreams will not ever be fulfilled; in fact, one of the things we give up at old age, or perhaps sooner, is that there is plenty of change but not much progress, except in certain areas. It's not true that everything is a contrast, good and evil, right and wrong. The universe is an experience without explanation; life, the fact of it, cannot be explained. When we reach old age, we have to start giving up some of our hopes.

In old age we realize that we *can't* change the universe.

Though we may make a great impact on a small part of it, even that impact needs to be seen as part of the overall unknown. We don't have the capacity to really understand life and the universe, but there are ways in which we express that lack of understanding — through poetry, music, and art — which resist interpretation, and are a mystery we are creating.

When we are young we still hope that we will find the stone of wisdom. We spend all our life trying to crack open the secret of life, and in the process we have learned and invented an amazing amount of knowledge, amassed so much of it and changed the face of the Earth. We never discover the secret of the universe and scramble along blindly, creating havoc, but also much beauty. We are searching, forever driven by a need to know and create — busy like the little ants.

From my window I see two highways. Day and night, thousands of cars travel back and forth and above them is the beauty and mystery of the unknown -- the stars, the sun and moon, but we rarely notice this. I have lived on this planet for 87 years but have not come any closer to the questions I have been asking every day of my life. "What is this life, this universe, all about?" Now I really know deep in my heart that I will never know the answer.

I'm trying to use or find a perspective that isn't usually used – I think this older old age outlives our framework of definitions. I've always had this feeling that I don't belong and that I can't really interpret the mystery because I don't have the capacity for thinking beyond the three familiar dimensions. With old age we realize that our future is limited. We can't the fix world. And of course this is a definition of death, the ultimate finality of fate.

There's no definition of where I am in life now. It's beyond old -- and I can't write about it because I can't define it. I'm saying goodbye to the last stage that's definable. I have never felt this way before. I'm living in a twilight world. In your younger years, you can go through life considering your future; but in old age there is no more future to imagine. How can you live without the future?

Maybe being beyond old forces us to really understand that the mystery is a reality. What stretches beyond the door of death is an eternity of unknown. Eternity and infinity are concepts that young children often struggle with, but soon give up because they can't find the answer. During our active lifetime we forget about it, and get so involved with day-to-day living that we don't see the mysterious universe in which we are trying to put our feet on some kind of concrete ground. Living beyond old, with our eyes open, may force us to truly accept the reality of the infinite and eternal, as well as to continue to understand the fact that we can never really know the answer while we are on this earth.

So, peeking around the door of death, I see the road to eternity and infinity as the reality I need to live now. From traveling miles and miles of earthly road, I will need to accept the unknown not only as the past and the present, but also as my only future. So my conclusion is that when you reach the age of "beyond old", your only reality is the unknown, but yet this has actually always been true. (We don't know the past or truly even the present.) We don't know whether what we feel as a Self, while we are alive, will remain as such or transform into further unknowns. Integrating these understandings as a reality may be the definition of "beyond old age."

Much has been said and written and researched about gifted children. Gifted adolescents also have a place in the consciousness of researchers. But it seems that there is a dearth of information when it comes to the gifted adult and giftedness in old age has not, as yet, caught our attention as a worthwhile subject of investigation. All elders have the task of keeping their minds carefully trained, and to keep on using them.

Keeping a sharp mind becomes a way of preserving one's independence and control. Just as I consciously watch every step I take so that I can keep control of my body and won't fall; I watch every thought I think, so that I can keep control of my daily life. There is a point at which we must give up that control, and the only people to whom we can trustingly give it up are those who love us unconditionally.

But the need for control is also a form of mistrust. If we look at our whole life experience, and especially that of young children, we will find that often we impose our own agenda on them; the same is true for old people. In rereading this article, I realize that I have accepted unconditionally the modern concept of old age. Namely, that there is really no place in our bustling reality (as we see it) for it. We become seniors, not the wise elders whose advice is sought and respectfully listened to. We put seniors into retirement homes. In fact, their children put them there. They are often not considered fully responsible anymore.

There are those who feel the burden of responsibility for them and gladly turn it over to their loving children and, of course, that should be respectfully accepted. But I am sure there are many who have accumulated much wisdom but no one asks their advice. Congress does not have a section for elders. You don't hear the elder's advice. Occasionally, one hears of elder statesmen, but we have no official place for them. We don't hear in Congress, "The 'elder' stateswoman from Hawaii wishes to speak."

What would happen if every administration had an elected council of elder states-people? Of course, they may have the same limitations as others but chances are that there may be a spiritual dimension, a view from the greater distance. Most of all, there is less of a personal agenda because they have lived their life and done their work.

What opportunities do we miss by not hearing our elders and what heightened experiences do they miss by not playing their appropriate role in society? How much wisdom goes down the drain unused? In personal terms, I probably have more opportunity to be heard because I am still active in my work with gifted children and I am listened to because my knowledge is defined and specific. Let us just remember how many parents and grandparents take care of their grandchildren or great-grandchildren. They are the unsung heroes and may have much wisdom to offer.

I am very curious about what is still ahead of me. I've spent quite a bit of thought on this wall that I'm coming up against — the wall of Death. I even have an image in my mind of what it looks like. I have the feeling I want to peek around it. Thinking about all this has all of a sudden opened a new door for me. And that door allows me to think that I must accept things as they are, without judgment. I must look at my own body not as old and aged, but that it is the way it is. And when I do that, I must see it as okay, and then I can realize that there is a beauty in old age, and that even an old body has its form of beauty. I must learn to apply to old people what I apply to children with whom I have worked; namely, that they are okay and beautiful in themselves, and it's only when we judge them against others that we find them wanting.

It's not death that bothers me,

but dying.

\- Annemarie Roeper

"Look, Ma! No Wrinkles!"
Annemarie, Age 92
In a playful mood

SHOCK AND OLD AGE

There are many years when life seems to be rather predictable and predetermined -- when we have chosen our life's work, when we have raised our children and when things have taken a normal course of development. This is also a time when people tend to predict what the future might be and have a certain security in that knowledge of predictability.

But then, and I don't know at what point that happens, much of what we have taken for granted breaks down and new standards and expectations have to develop. For years, I used to know what to expect of my life and my relationships. The school my husband George and I founded in Michigan followed a certain pattern. My children grew up along the normal developmental lines. We had become rather well known in the field of gifted education and George and I were often in demand for speaking engagements. We were well thought of and very respected by our community.

I really don't know at which point the situation changed. It altered over time and in every respect. One day we weren't being asked to give keynote speeches anymore. We were no longer perceived as the people who had the knowledge and the psychological background of helping the gifted child. And then slowly, without noticing it myself; and of course particularly after George died and I was alone, things began to change again. Even though I had been the first person to be chosen to represent gifted education in the Legacy Series by the (NAGC) National Association for Gifted Children, I moved into a different level of recognition.

Now I truly don't know what to expect for my own future in every respect – where to live, what to do, whether to continue working to still earn some money, whether to sell my house. I am at a total crossroads and because I am a creative thinker and very observant, I am aware of every step and every pitfall that I am encountering. I truly don't know what choices a 90-year-old woman with a good mind and a handicap in walking and hearing still has at her disposal.

I am now in a retirement home. This was a shock even though it somehow seemed the next step that I should take. I'm still not sure a retirement home (or "assisted living community" as they call it now) is the right place for me. I need to be involved in more intellectual activity and purposeful work and find myself spending too much time just sleeping and eating. Being needed has always been the center of my life, whether it was just the school, my children or my friends. I guess what I am expressing now is the voice of depression and desperation and loneliness. I don't know what to do. I know that I still have a lot to offer, I just don't know which way to go. I know there are people who make their best contribution at 90!

It's a shock to lose our homes, our work, and our position in society. Somehow we just need someone to say to us:

"We need you." to rediscover our purpose and to feel that we are wanted.

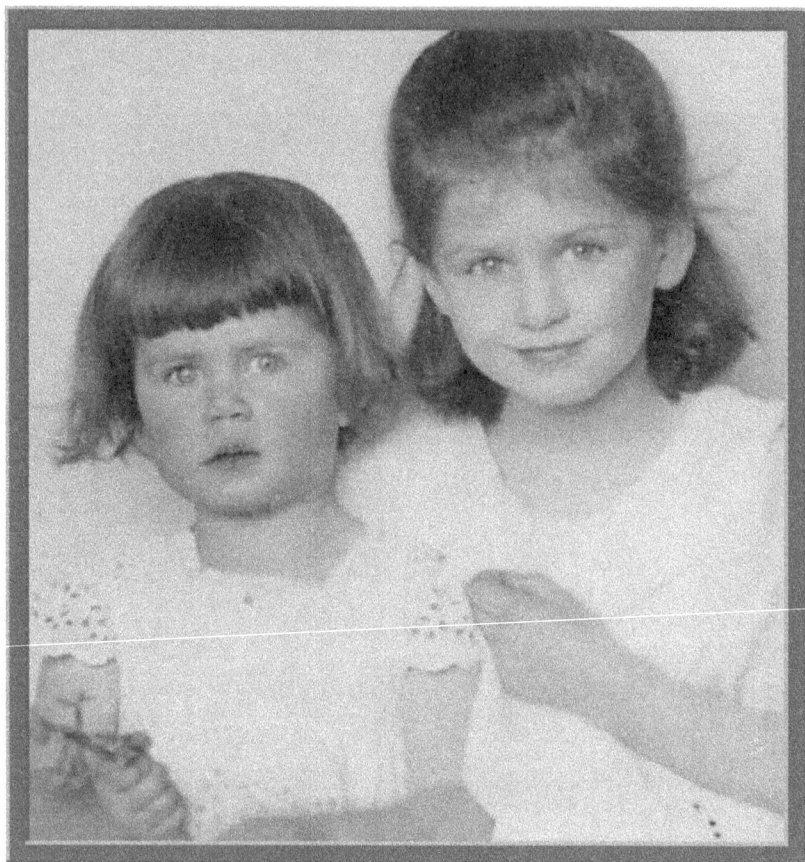

ANNEMARIE, AGE 6
AND HER SISTER, ULLA, AGE 3

APPROACHING
100 YEARS OF LIVING
WITH AWARENESS

Right now I am entering the year in which I will be 90 years old. Imagine! I am, surely, beyond old. Yet, I recently had a conversation with a friend about how I might celebrate the occasion of my 100th birthday. We will see, there is time enough to consider that.

Thinking back over the past year, I feel that one of the things that has made this an important year for me is that I was nominated by the NAGC (National Association for Gifted Children) to be the first honoree in a series called, "Portraits in Gifted Education: The Legacy Series." This was established to interview and videotape notable educators, researchers, leaders and advocates. I was deeply touched by this honor, partly on a personal level and partly because it signifies a more general acceptance of giftedness as a set of emotional characteristics as well as the more familiar cognitive ones.

I'm kind of eager to share my thoughts, feelings and experiences with you, and I don't know where to begin. Approaching 90 years old, I find myself in a new phase of life. I truly don't know where I belong. I imagine that this feeling is typical for people my age: there is no defined category for us to fit into. There is a place for children and parents, a place for adulthood, for grandparents -- but what comes after that is largely unexplored territory. There is no question that I am nearing the end of my life, but I realize that I am the same person that I was at the beginning. I feel that I see the world, my Self, and my relationship to the environment through the same eyes that I was born with.

A few years ago, I wrote a book, <u>The 'I' of the Beholder</u>. That same "I" looks out on the world today as it did 90 ago. I imagine I have learned from life's experiences, yet I feel that I'm not inherently wiser. I am perhaps wiser experientially, but not wiser in the sense of heart and soul. I believe that a newborn infant holds all the wisdom that he or she will ever have. In fact, there is an enormous richness that exists in the inner life of the infant. There is no more passionate love than the love of the baby for its mother and father. All future loves grow out of this one, and one's whole life is flavored by this original relationship. In fact, I believe that feelings never shine as brilliantly as they do in the young child. Feelings soon become jaded and changed by ambitions and goals and by the belief that we need to do the reasonable thing, whatever that may be for every individual. But maybe I have reached a point in my life where I don't have to be reasonable anymore. I'm free to do anything I want. Is that good? I don't know. In some ways it is frightening.

But that is the fantasy; that is the imagination. In reality, I'm more restricted than I've ever been. There are more fences and more "No Trespassing" signs in my life, not because someone or something is stopping me, but because I'm not physically able. Then there are the prejudices against old age, which you come across every step of the way. "Does she take sugar in her coffee?" a waiter asked my companion, evidently thinking that I didn't have the capacity to hear or answer for myself. And yet, I realize that this may not be true for everybody my age. My mind is as sharp as ever, there isn't much that I miss, but there is little I can do about that prejudice.

I used to have such high hopes. I used to think that my task was to change the world. That is why George and I founded a school, after the enormous disappointment we had in having to flee Germany because of the Nazis. We wanted to give children a solid sense of Self and a commitment to justice and community so that what the Nazis did would never occur again. We may have made a difference for some of our students and for our own three children, but I must realize that in the long run my very existence will be forgotten, and probably that is as it should be.

And yet, there is continuity. Life itself is continuous: my great grandchildren will carry some of my DNA, but also that which has come to them through an unknown, distant past. Of course, we are living in a world filled with turmoil, as it always has been, but life itself is a miracle; and the joy we can give each other, to support each other, is a miracle in itself.

As I look at everything that has been given me, I am filled with gratitude. As I age, I know that with my children and also many of my friends, the roles have been reversed. I've become the recipient, rather than the giver, of love and care. I realize that this is my task for the few years I am still around: to learn to receive, hoping and believing that I can trust my environment to continue to support my independence of thought and decision making, even if I can't continue to live as independently as I have up to this point.

I realize that it's not up to me, and never was, to change the world. Maybe I can still make a tiny contribution, but perhaps for myself and for my own enjoyment as much if not more than the benefit of the world. My task is to deal with my own death in a courageous manner. At this moment, I'm the oldest person that I know, and I know I will be carried to the end on the wings of love of all those who care for me.

ANNEMARIE
IN BODEGA BAY, CALIFORNIA

CROSSING A LINE

Always in life we are confronted with the mystery of the unknown, and at the end of life the unknown fills up more and more of our inner space.

In my life's experience and particularly in my career as an educator, I did not expect that there would be anything I hadn't anticipated or lived through before. Each time a big transition came into my life, it proved to be a challenge that I enjoyed and mastered. So it actually came as a surprise to me when I reached the age of 92 – of what I call "beyond old age" -- that I felt that a moment had arrived when I was at a total loss to know where I was going.

My life had been a very active one and it was based on the premise that I had something to offer, especially to children. My husband and I founded and ran the Roeper School for Gifted Children, in Michigan, for 40 years. In a long career like that there are ups and downs and failures and successes, but in general I felt fulfilled by my work and by the realization that I was actually making a difference by helping many children and their parents. Most of all we developed a philosophy ("The Roeper Philosophy") based on the premise that every person has an obligation to make this world a better place -- in other words that one needs to think beyond the fulfillment of one's own destiny. I felt we were successful in fulfilling our goals. The Roeper School, which was the container that allowed this philosophy to blossom, is still in existence today.

If I really think about it, that is the reason why I find myself in my present position of crossing a line. There is no true definition of this stage of life in our society. At this point, my world expects me to have fulfilled my destiny and that I am no longer needed to make any contributions. Everything that my late husband and I created, which of course includes my wonderful and growing family as well as the school, is doing well without us. Beyond being a mother, a grandmother, a great-grandmother and a friend to many people, there is no real social definition of what or who I should be at this point. My work is done and the world clearly goes on without me, but where does that leave me?

The fact that the roles are reversed now and that adult children take care of their elderly parents is of course a good and necessary one. Personally, I have maintained the strict expectation that no decisions are going to be made about me without me, but I think this is where another transition takes place. There is a feeling that even though nobody has taken the power of attorney away from the elderly, that now their children are responsible for them. Out of this grew the idea of creating a specific place for the elderly – the concept of retirement homes. This is of course a logical consequence, but how does this really feel to those who are now residents in them?

In Israel at least some years ago there was a principle that everyone of every age was able to contribute and was required to do so. I remember from a visit there years ago, an old woman who could actually not walk anymore, sitting in front of the cupboards and organizing the clean linen to be used by the community. She had an important job to do. The cupboards were arranged so that she could do her work sitting down.

Maybe even in retirement homes people should be required to fulfill certain duties, up to the extent they were able to, as a condition of becoming a member. This would give them a purpose and a useful activity. If they did things like that, these would be very different places. Many old people have a great deal of wisdom and a lot to offer. To isolate them in retirement homes and to not take advantage of their accumulated experience is a disservice to them and to their community. We should try to do something about it.

The fact is that in our society we do cross a line at some point, where people perceive us differently and assume we can't be useful any more. The reality is that people don't really change. Old people have the same desires, feelings and needs for affection and purpose as do younger people. They don't want to be ignored, but most of all, they are not eager to be put on pedestals and be admired

– they want to still count as useful human beings – and they are in many ways!

There are few alternatives offered the elderly in our society. There should be a counsel of elders available to advise Congress. The fact that they are no longer actively involved adds to their ability to make unbiased contributions. It is for this reason that even at 92 I have never really stopped working or being available to help gifted children and adults.

What I realize is that there is now only one last line to contemplate -- between the known and the unknown. When we are confronted with death, that final line, we have to truly integrate into our feeling and thinking that we *don't* know what happens next. In the end, embracing this mystery affects how we live our life at any age.

ANNEMARIE
AND HANNELE BARUSCHKE,
BEST FRIEND AND CLASSMATE
AT MARIENAU, GERMANY
EARLY 1930S

BEYOND 92: LOSING YOUR INDEPENDENCE

As I see it now, losing my independence is the most frustrating and debilitating part of aging. You realize there are certain things you can't do anymore. I personally have been very aware of that and have anticipated the moments of deterioration of ability. Some people will not recognize that and it has to be taken away from them, which is much harder. It is difficult to give up driving. It is difficult to be told by your relatives, "I don't want you to drive my children anymore."

Knowing when you can't do something anymore and acting upon that knowledge voluntarily is difficult for anybody. For someone who has always been in total control of themselves it can be a very complicated emotional maneuver. It not only involves trusting other people to know something about you better than you know yourself, but also believing that you know best. I don't know if you ever get used to this because certain things only you can know. Only I can know where the shoe hurts. It becomes a very difficult situation for those who love you and want to see you safe and happy and to realize that there are certain things you can't do anymore.

It is a delicate interaction and I think I have been going through this process for a long time. Pride and self-esteem are deeply involved in this and actually I don't know that I can really write about this because I have not solved the problem for myself. It is my belief that I should be in total control of my destiny as much as it is in my hands and I do believe that a person has the right to destroy him or herself if that is what they want to do. I think the limit comes in where they might be doing harm to other people. Especially between loving family members, this stage of life becomes a very subtle give and take that requires enormous sensitivity.

It is a two-way street. As you age, you become by necessity more dependent. You have to also consider the needs of your loved ones as well as your own. That is easily said and difficult to do as one ages. One needs to forego so many pleasures – for example: missing the wedding of my niece who was married on a boat on the Hudson River with all the relatives including my two great grandchildren participating. The only one who couldn't be there was me because the event was too difficult to get to.

The discrepancy between wants and hopes and the ability to actually do them gets greater as time goes on. There is a period right now where around me people of all ages are getting married and it always leaves me with a feeling of sadness that I can't do that anymore, although I probably could! The need for a close relationship remains unchanged. In many cases, the best experiences, both physical and emotional, happen in old age.

ANNEMARIE
& GEORGE ROEPER
AT ROEPER SCHOOL
FOR GIFTED CHILDREN
1970

THOUGHTS ON OLD AGE

How does old age find its place in a world that is already so mysterious that we have no way of really grasping it? To be so close to dying and to know there is no escape makes it a strange and wondrous place to be.

All we know is the reality in which we live and at this point in my life it is dominated by mundane considerations such as: incontinence, difficulty walking and little pains and hurts. It seems like this takes over totally and the world in which you live shrinks. My life is behind me; my future is behind me, except for the last bit of future that is awaiting me unavoidably. I look out the window and it looks like it always did except that the world won't be there anymore after a few more years because the only world that exists is the one that you experience. You live in a reality, and this is the only one you know.

But it is probably as unreal as anything else. 'I think,

therefore I am,' said Descartes. I must look at that quote again from the vantage point of old age. I am because it is all I know and, yet, knowledge is fantasy as much as everything else.

What is ahead of me now is even more unknown than the past. In the past, the ideas I had created a reality for myself that was familiar and part of me, but that reality is disappearing and disintegrating and now all that is left is a step into the unknown – a step from existence to non-existence. That is a concept that is not really a concept because we can't imagine what it is like to not exist. And yet, it is the only reality when we reach this age.

It doesn't really matter if you've lived a good life or not. If I were able to think in terms of doing good deeds so I could get into heaven, my feelings about life would be so simple and I wouldn't have to have any fear. But as it is, the mystery becomes bigger the older I get and I live in a vacuum of not knowing. Maybe there is something there if we do exist -- we have a daily life, we eat and we love and we have sex and we experience it all with deep feeling but it, too, is nothing but fantasy. More and more I think that the reality is non-existent. Maybe all that exists is imagination, a glowing something we don't yet know, but passionately pursue, even though it may not be real.

Maybe one of my goals should be to come up with a description of non-existence. Existence only interferes with that which we don't know. This is just playing with words as I have done so much in my life. Goethe, the famous German poet, said something like, "A name is nothing but noise and smoke. It isn't really there." All I know is that there is a growing circle of nothingness that surrounds me more than ever in my life. Hopefully it includes other people, because in the end the only reality is love.

ANNEMARIE

AGE 15

IN PRAISE OF FANTASY

There is another subject that I want to write about and this is the healing quality of the imagination. The one thing that is at our disposal is our fantasy and our imagination and it goes in all directions, especially when there are things that are otherwise unobtainable to us.

I think many loves and desires, which are not responded to, become bearable because we can imagine that which can't be happening in reality and it comes close to the same satisfaction. The little boy who has to submit to his father's demands can say, "if you make me do this, I'll break your house down and I will run away from home and do all sorts of things." The imagined power relieves some of the pain of being powerlessness.

How to deal with or obtain the unobtainable is the same theme as growing older. I think the world is filled with unfulfilled dreams, which make the reality more acceptable. This is a subject that one could write much more about. Imagination, of course, is the basis of the world of children, who can invent so many things. The invention of the unobtainable often leads to the obtainable. You may actually someday build your dream house or live with the person you desire.

As I age, I am learning more and more about the power of imagination. Most adults don't understand why children often don't pay attention. They are occupied with things that are more real to them and probably more important. The child who doesn't listen to the teacher and follows a bird outside the window imagines what this bird might be seeing on his travels. He learns much more than the teacher could teach him.

Even though I never went to college, I was able to educate myself with freedom in a stimulating environment filled with art and music, literature and travel. It allowed me to learn more than many people do during years of study who are forced to concentrate on what they are being told to do rather than on what they desire to do. In my case, unstructured learning turned out to be more useful than an organized educational process. Schools, of course, fulfill a very necessary function; and I am not implying that they are not needed.

We learn to walk and talk and eat and chew and many other things without anybody teaching us. The most important things in life, we learn by ourselves by watching others. This brings with it the desire for specific learning, which requires the help of other people, such as learning how to drive a car (although some people learn to drive on their own). The best learning we do is because we desire it, encouraged by a stimulating and loving environment. The imagination is one of our greatest tools.

As we age, we age unevenly. Our ability to walk may deteriorate, while our brains might function as well as ever. The asynchronicity between our dreams and desires and our ability to fulfill them also grows greater as we grow older. The most difficult change we have to accept is losing some of our independence and the need to rely on others. It is very important to realize that, in contrast, the imagination does not age. By necessity, it takes over more and more of the reality to which we are accustomed. We have to re-learn to accept dependency as we did when we were young. This is an enormous sacrifice for someone who has spent most of his or her adult life being able to rely on themselves. It is at this point where the imagination becomes of serious importance.

Even memory is really imagination because it is needed to help us recreate the past. I have often heard it said that some people live in the past and might spend hours seemingly lost in what used to be. This is often perceived in kind of a disdainful way. There is a saying, "He doesn't live in reality anymore, he only lives in the past." Often there isn't much reality to live in for old people, or it isn't pleasant, and the past is the preferred reality.

We probably aren't aware of what importance the imagination is for everybody, but particularly how necessary it is for old people. At old age, you are limited in what you can still do or accomplish. This is not really universally true because there are many people who are productive until the very end, even though it may take a different form. Aging often means learning to compensate for what we can't do anymore. Imagination is one way that helps us compensate.

Along with the imagination, I think that feelings don't age. I still find an attractive man attractive. Interests don't age either. I love traveling as I always did. In old age, we realize that there is much we have missed in the world that we might have enjoyed or experienced. If we have the capacity to dream, we can imagine what it would have been like had we experienced it. We are able to substitute fantasy for experience to some extent, albeit in a very small way.

We spend much of our life replacing reality with the imagination. This is evident by the way in which we identify with the stories that we experience through reading or television or listening to music. It is true not just in old age, but all through life. We are always supplementing our real life experiences through identification with what we read or see or hear about. Our life's reality is totally intertwined with the life of fantasy.

The media take advantage of this need in human beings. This is really how theater and movies and now the internet play such an enormous role in our daily living. Fantasy is an essential part of reality. How empty our life would be without our capacity for fantasy! This is so true for everybody.

Imagination is one of the most unrecognized learning tools in our world. The child who plays house is predicting and learning something about what his or her future life will be like. By the same token, when you are old, you are re-imagining some of your life experiences. The difference is that in old age you are also imagining what it will be like after this experience here on earth.

All through life, we are dreaming about the future or hoping for certain events to happen. That is still true in old age. The greatest unknown is death, but imagination doesn't really answer the question of existence. I think what we do is use the imagination as kind of a counterfeit because we can't live with the fact that we simply don't know the answers. We invent them and imagination serves that purpose very well.

Some of these questions do not exist for people who are deeply involved in their religious beliefs. In some ways it is easier to be religious. Life is taken care of and death is taken care of when you have a strong faith. Religion absolves us of a great deal of anxiety. Some people may know the answers to what life and death are, but I do not. I believe in the mystery. The mystery is my religion and this includes all beliefs or no belief. I have learned to live with not knowing. When I imagine the end of life, I imagine a wall that I can't penetrate. Sometimes I think I can peek around the corner and see what's behind the wall, but I'm not sure I can do that. I think everybody is afraid of the unknown, whether they are religious or not.

Fantasy helps us overcome some of the hurdles of not knowing. It helps us fill some of the holes of unfulfilled desires, like potholes in a deteriorating street. It makes it possible for us to live with unbearable loss and pain. Hooray for fantasy!

George & Annemarie, 1940

George & Annemarie, 1985

THE FINAL STEP

The concept of dying requires understanding the concept of living.

I feel now that I need to create a platform from which to take this plunge into the unknown, but that might be predicated on the idea that I would like to do it all in a most pleasant and proper way. When I think about it, it is because I feel that I want control over my living and dying. It might actually be the very thing that I should not be trying to achieve, because it is the letting go, the letting happen, the total sinking into the unknown that is something I need to achieve.

I keep having the image of the baby that is being held by his or her parent – in fact, I am remembering holding my own babies and I remember that when I didn't hold them tight enough and they felt like falling, they were frightened. They needed that help and support. In a way you need it all your life, but I am getting closer to the moment where I have to understand that the last step into the unknown has to be taken all by myself.

I am in a strange situation now because I feel that there have been many factors involved in preparation for this step. Ironically at 90, I am now building a new life. I am having to use the skills that I have learned in daily living in my interaction with other people and yet I am still concerned with aspects of reality such as: money, where do I live, and how do I live, how my life will continue to be structured and what will be my environment. My real present environment is but a small part of the unknown in which we all really live.

It used to be predictable how the week would proceed and now I am taking a step out of all of that, which creates much anxiety, much regret of losing what I've had and much fear of the future. It fuels the desire to really have a clear image of my whole past.

I have always wanted to share things with my friends and the world around me – and that maybe one reason we have friends is because in one way they are a mirror of ourselves. I would like to understand myself through their reactions to me and their interest in me. But mostly I think we need to feel the genuine love for who we are and a real acceptance and respect for even that which we don't understand about each other.

What happens when you become beyond old is that you become again an unknown unit, like you were when you were born. That is the biggest problem and I am hoping I can keep my identity without all the trimmings I am used to having around it, such things as: being honored for the person who is best known in the field of gifted education, and co-creating and running the Roeper School for Gifted Children for all those years.

This writing is kind of my farewell letter in a way. I believe that I have lived a good life. Despite many challenges, I continue to live a good life. And now, I want to die a good death.

ANNEMARIE, AGE 89
EL CERRITO, CALIFORNIA

THE LAST OF
A GENERATION

I think I am in mourning, mourning a generation, mourning a life both good and bad, mourning the past, mourning the fact that I have no future, mourning my own upcoming death. There will be no more morning glories. There will be no glories at all.

A few days after my husband George died, my good friend and colleague Linda Silverman and I decided we wanted to take a little trip. The only lodgings we could find were at a Buddhist monastery called Green Gulch north of San Francisco, which had guest rooms. When I told them that my husband had just died, they asked if I'd had a ceremony and I said "no." We devoted the next day to George. The monks began chanting. What they were chanting most of the time was, 'Nothingness. Nothingness. Nothingness.' Somehow that meant a lot to me. It was a strange thing that we happened to spend the night at a Buddhist temple.

Here is the poem I wrote for him a while later:

THE PURE SWEETNESS OF MOURNING

For the past year since George's death

my feelings have traveled through new vistas,

places I had never been, deep valleys of disbelief,

mountains of guilt and doubt, rivers of memories

running joyfully over stones and branches,

moving slowly over unexplored crevices.

All was judgment.

There was thunder and lightning,

peaceful sunshine and cloudless skies

and frequent deep fog.

An ocean separated me from the level of dailiness –

my new landscape was so deep inside me.

How could I cross this ocean?

Was there a bridge?

But I began to be familiar

with my landscape of mourning

And I began to love it.

The guilt and doubt slowly fell away.

Mourning has now taken over the space next to me.

Through mourning George is at my side again

Where he belongs.

Mourning has become my bridge to daily life.

For now there is no betrayal of the past,

And my tears, which would not stop as I wrote,

Were tears of joyful sadness.

Could you feel it with me just a little?

I'm mourning a whole generation. I'm mourning all the
people who don't live anymore. Maybe I am mourning my
past, my life that I can never have back again. After
George died, I never wanted to stop mourning and I felt a
loss when I all of a sudden realized that I had, but now I

am mourning my own death and the fact that there is no future for me anymore. There is just a little future, and I might enjoy it, but now my task is to learn how to die. I have talked about the unknown so much – the unknown is so known to me -- it is always present in my life, but now it is going to be the reality, the future of my life. No matter how you think about it, there is not going to be much more and I keep thinking that I want to do it right. I want to die the proper way.

But there is just a little slice of life left and how I will use it I don't know. I'd like to use it well and I'd like to enjoy it and I'd like to feel the beauty of my loves and my relationships. I have never been one who gets lost in reminiscing because I always have been forward looking and I think that is what I am doing now – trying to figure out what is coming up for me. There is a strange sadness, but that is also because I am the last of a generation and a whole new cycle is starting and I will not be part of it.

There are millions of people who've died, so it is not

unusual at all, it is not a new experience, but it will be for me. I am feeling a heaviness and a lightness at the same time. I think it is the knowledge that this end is coming. There is a word about there being nothing I can do from keeping it from happening – inevitability.

I think that is what I feel I am occupying myself with now -- looking into the future that is not the future, to really experience the end of life. I'm wondering if there will be nothing but darkness. I think religious people think that there will be nothing but light. Maybe it will be a light darkness or a heavy light. It will be maybe be a new adventure and that might be the best way to look at it – the adventure of not having a future.

ANNEMARIE
AN AGELESS 92

BETWEEN THIS WORLD
AND THE NEXT

Ninety-two – that is my new age and I'm trying hard to get used to it. It's about this time in life where one of the important transitions takes place, similar to moving from adolescence to adulthood.

Life is definitely behind me, life as I've known it. I will, of course, never have any more children, I will never drive a car again, I will never co-found a school again, and I could go on and on with the 'never, ever agains.' I am also out of the circle of work that I've been involved in. I am rarely asked to give speeches anymore and although people still seek my advice, it has become rare in relation to what used to be.

In the place I am now, I feel the admiration and the love of many people who feel they've benefited from some of the work that I've done through my life. To be truthful, I know I have impacted many lives and that impact is carried on in future generations and I feel grateful for having had that opportunity. Most of all, my family is growing in America. I have great-grandchildren and some of what George and I have conveyed to them by our own living has become implanted in them and their lives go on. Knowing this is an amazing and happy feeling, but I have yet to find my new place in the world.

I was born in 1918. The last few days around my birthday, August 27th, I have been surrounded by the love of many people. Some came from far away to celebrate with me. All this has been more deeply gratifying than anyone can imagine. Simultaneously, it is about the time for the 100th anniversary of George's birth and even though it has been many years since he has left me, we have really been intertwined a great part of my life, actually since I was 11 years old, when we first met and fell in love at Marienau, the school my parents founded in Germany.

But it is not the history of that relationship that I want to describe at this moment. I want to talk about what it feels like to be more and more out of the circle of living and working and experiencing that I've been doing most of my life. I am feeling that I am going through another of those great transitions that we experience, or that come upon us almost unexpectedly, such as adolescence and marriage and children. Those are times that bring a finality with them, I think, although they are vastly different in each person's fate and experience.

What I'm trying to incorporate in my emotional life just now is this last stage -- this transitional stage from life to death. I do feel with gratitude that I lived my life well and that the many years that George and I shared were like two trees intertwined. Even though I am sure there were mistakes that I've made and things that I could have done differently, I am basically satisfied with what I've had and what I've done, but also extremely grateful for all the support and love that I have experienced, even after George died and I had to get used to living by myself.

Awareness of the unknown has always been a part of my life, but that that may now be the only world for me. It will be the time when my feeling of Self dissolves into the universe. This it the point where many people disagree with me. I feel that the soul, the Self, is caught inside the human or animal being, like in a cocoon that both protects it and restricts it.

For 92 years, I have been comfortable in the cocoon and now the point has come that I need to break through it and wonder how that will happen. It seems to me that what death really is, is the dissolution of your defined Self. I am not a believer in an afterlife or that I will meet everybody that I've once loved again in a new world. I believe there will be no "I" in its accustomed form. It seems to me that many people I know believe that they will reappear in some way under different and maybe better circumstances. I don't know how much truth there is in this belief. I feel that we have come from the unknown and that we are going back to the unknown and it is the greatest transition for any living being, possibly into nothingness. It is this transition that I want to be able to accept and deal with honestly and without fear and maybe this would be my farewell message at my memorial celebration.

I've always thought that when I die many people will react with some sadness, people all over the world that I have known. It feels like a sinking boat. A boat sinks and it might fall to the bottom of the sea and it creates at first enormous waves – big, big waves all around it – much commotion and much noise. And as time goes on, the waves go further and further, but become calmer and calmer. Finally my soul will settle on the ground of the universe and the waters will quiet down. There will still be a few ripples and after a while the waters will smoothe and my soul will rest or disappear back into its original parts and rhythm.

I don't know if my existence will have had an impact on the world, but I hope that I have done my part to change some things for the better. Actually, probably the real words for this are, or the reality is, that I will continue to exist in the memory of people and the fact that I have changed lives.

I have born three children, have three grandchildren and soon will have three great-grandchildren.

An important factor that I will never forget and is that this family was destined to die under the German Nazis. We were meant to disappear from this earth and now, our Selves, our knowledge, our DNA will continue in this world and the line will go on for generations.

I feel that that is a great part of my legacy and something that will allow me to die a peaceful death. I guess I want to end this with the expression of the abundance of love that I feel for so many -- for my own children, my grandchildren and great-grandchildren and all the friends that have surrounded me with so much love.

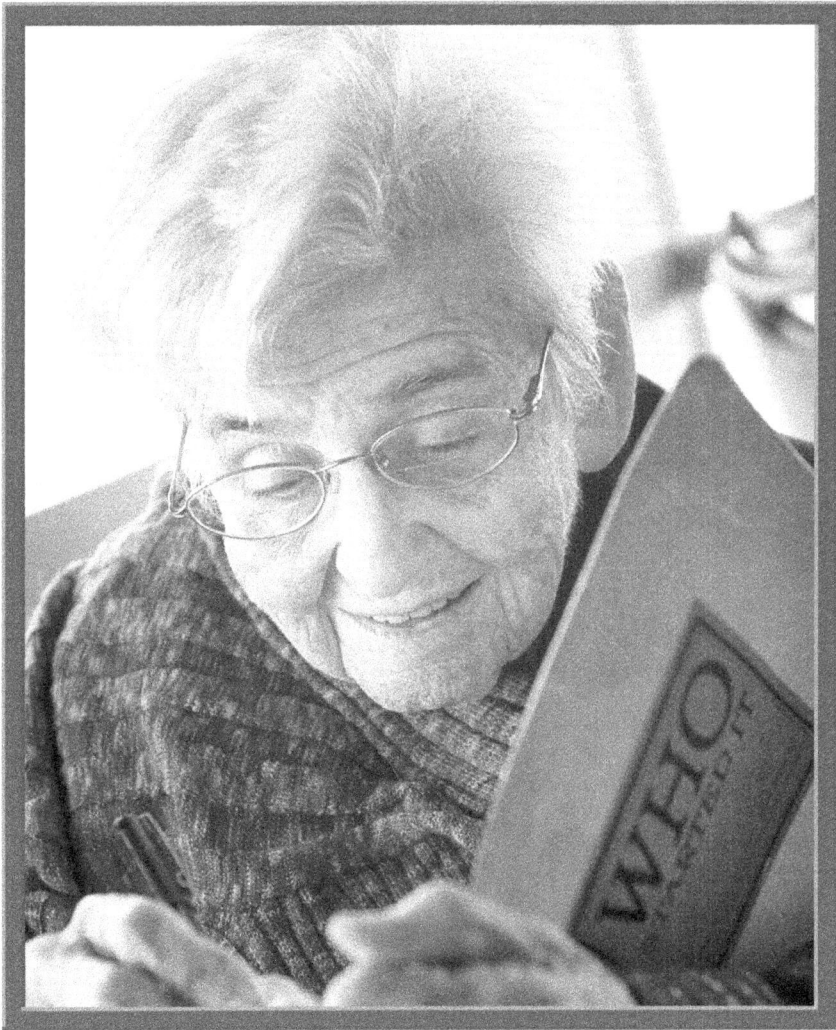

ANNEMARIE
SIGNING ONE OF HER
FOUR CHILDREN'S BOOKS

ABOUT THE AUTHOR

Annemarie Roeper, Ed.D. is an educational consultant with more than 60 years of specializing in the needs of gifted and creative children and adults. In 1941, she and her husband, George, founded the Roeper School for Gifted Children in Michigan, one of the nation's oldest and best-known progressive private schools for gifted young people.

Annemarie was born in Austria in 1918. Her father, Max Bondy, was a noted art historian and educator. Her mother, Gertrud Wiener Bondy, who studied with Sigmund Freud, was the first female psychoanalyst in Europe. Annemarie had begun studies with Sigmund and Anna Freud when the Nazis forced her family to flee, leaving behind the school they had created near Hamburg, Germany called Marienau.

Dr. Roeper's life and contribution to education has been documented in the book, "The 'I' of the Beholder," in the film "Across

Time and Space" and many other books, essays and articles. In 2007, she was chosen as the first to be videotaped in the NAGC's 'Portraits in Gifted Education: The Legacy Series.' At 92 years of age, she continues to be active writing books and essays and working with gifted children and adults.

Annemarie welcomes your letters, emails and thoughts about her work.

RESOURCES & CURRENT PUBLICATIONS BY ANNEMARIE ROEPER, ED.D.

BOOKS

I Need All My Teddy Bears
The Plane Went Down in Buffalo
Small & Tall
Who Started It?
Azalea Art Press, 2010.

Educating Children for Life:
The Modern Learning Community
Royal Fireworks Press, 1990.

The "I" of the Beholder:
A Guided Journey to the Essence of a Child
Great Potential Press, 2007.

My Life Experiences with Children:
Selected Writings and Speeches
Deleon Publishing, Inc., 2004.

ARTICLES

Living with Intensity
(2 Articles by Annemarie Roeper)
Edited by Susan Daniels, Ph.D.
& Michael M. Piechowski, Ph.D.
Great Potential Press, 2009.

FILMS

Across Time & Space
Kathryn Golden, Producer
Searchlight Films, 2002.

An Evening with Annemarie Roeper /
Portraits in Gifted Education: The Legacy Series
National Association for Gifted Children, 2008.

OTHER REFERENCES

A View from the Self:
A Life History of Annemarie Roeper
Michele Kane, Ed.D. / unpublished dissertation
Loyola University, Chicago, 2006.

Interview with Annemarie Roeper
Holocaust Oral History Project
San Francisco, CA, 1992.

Photo

CREDITS

Note From The Photographer:

When I was a little girl, my brother, sister and I used to fight a lot. To help us understand our feelings and behaviors, my Mom bought us a book titled <u>Who Started It</u>. The book really resonated with me, as I vividly remember the characters, the storyline and the images.

Forty-five years later, my friend Karen Mireau, an author, publisher, and biographer, told me that Dr. Roeper needed photos for her upcoming book of essays. Karen showed me a flyer listing Dr. Roeper's other books. There, to my surprise, was my childhood book!

Amazingly enough, my sister still owned the book and sent it to me. Dr. Roeper inscribed it on the day of our photo shoot and I could not have been more delighted! My siblings and I no longer push or hit each other. Maybe Dr. Roeper had something to do with that.

- Shoey Sindel

Shoey Sindel is a Berkeley based portrait, wedding, mitzvah and event photographer. She can be reached through her website www.shoeysindel.com and her blog www.clickchickblog.com.

Contact:

For More Information
& a Full bibliography Visit:

Http://RoeperConsultationService.
blogspot.com

Annemarie Roeper, Ed.D.
11889 Skyline Boulevard
Oakland . CA . 94619

Email Annemarie Roeper at:
amroeper @aol.com

For Inquiries
About the Publisher Visit:

Azalea Art Press
45 Alta Road
Berkeley . CA . 94708

AzaleaArtPress@Gmail.com

Http://AzaleaArtPress.
Blogspot.com

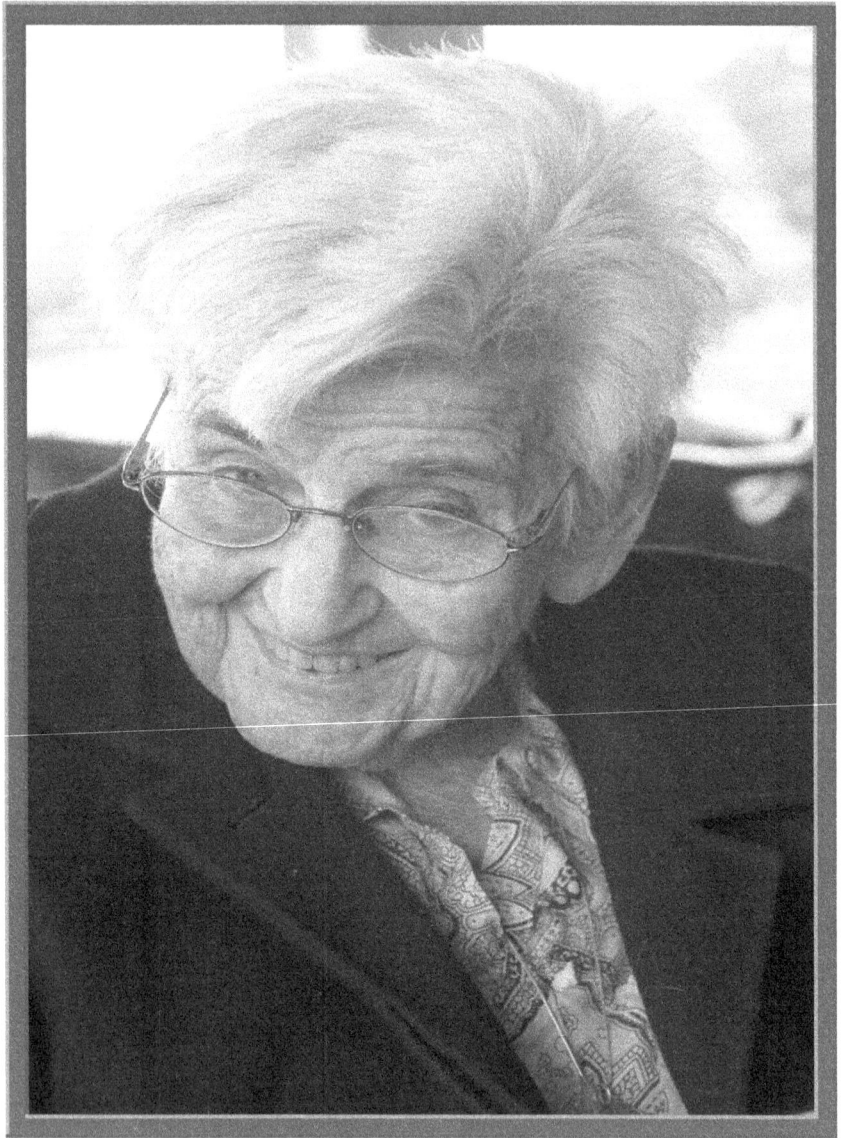

ANNEMARIE
BERKELEY, CALIFORNIA
2011

www.ingramcontent.com/pod-product-compliance
Lightning Source LLC
Chambersburg PA
CBHW022126280326
41933CB00007B/563